MARTIN SIMPSON

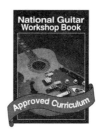

TEACHES ALTERNATE TUNINGS

A Systematic Approach to Open and Altered Tunings

MARTIN SIMPSON

Alfred, the leader in educational publishing, and the National Guitar Workshop,

one of America's finest guitar schools, have joined forces to bring you

the best, most progressive educational tools possible. We hope you will enjoy

this book and encourage you to look for other fine products from Alfred

and the National Guitar Workshop.

D1608831

This book was acquired, edited and produced
by Workshop Arts, Inc., the publishing arm of
the National Guitar Workshop.
Nathaniel Gunod, acquisitions, editor
Michael Rodman, editor
John Roberts, music typesetter
Timothy Phelps, interior design
Randy Anglin, cover photo

ISBN 0-7390-2346-2 (Book)
ISBN 0-7390-2402-7 (Book & DVD)

TABLE OF CONTENTS

INTRODUCTION

This book correlates to the video, *Martin Simpson Teaches Alternate Tunings*. It includes everything that is taught in the video and provides some extra background and some extra music to reinforce and support the material. There is a DVD available with this book that contains the complete original video. Together, the book and the DVD make a powerful learning tool for any guitarist interested in alternate tunings.

This book provides an overview of *open tunings* and *altered tunings*. Modern acoustic guitar playing is largely defined by players like Michael Hedges, Martin Carthy, Joni Mitchell and others—all of whom have used open tunings. An open tuning is one in which the open strings form a chord, generally either major or minor. Altered tunings are those which form more unusual chords, which themselves are generally considered alterations of basic chords, such as Gsus4 (an altered G Major chord) or Csus2 (an altered C Major chord).

We tend to think of open tunings as being rather modern and cutting edge, and in some ways they are. They've also been with us for a very long time. And if you were to go around the world right now and examine the use of tunings on the acoustic guitar, you might find that Open G or Open D tunings would be more widespread than "standard" tuning. I've played with guitar players from all over the world and found some tunings to be very commonly used by Malagasy musicians, Hindustani slide players, blues players from the Delta and Hawaiian guitarists. I find the same tunings again and again.

This book and DVD are designed to demystify how important open and altered tunings relate to each other and to standard tuning. Hopefully, by the time you have studied this material thoroughly, you'll be comfortable enough to experiment with these tunings and perhaps invent a few of your own. Enjoy.

ABOUT THE AUTHOR

Martin Simpson is one of the world's premiere acoustic guitarists and a powerful songwriter with a rich, charactered voice. His playing, which helped define the English steel-string acoustic guitar sound, is idiosyncratic, instantly recognizable and revered among guitar fans. His body of work is diverse, encompassing all types of traditional and acoustic music, and he has toured with everyone from June Tabor to Steve Miller.

When he was 22 he recorded his first album, *Golden Vanity*. The year the album came out (1976), Martin went on tour with Steeleye Span, opening for them in some of the biggest rock venues in England. He recorded three albums with June Tabor ("A Cut Above," "Abyssinians" and "Aquaba"). As his career progressed, Martin also worked with some of Britain's most accomplished musicians, including Martin Carthy, Dave Mattacks, Ashley Hutchings, Simon Nicol and Richard Thompson. His more recent work includes a number of recordings with his wife, poet, songwriter Jessica Radcliffe; recorded collaborations with Martin Carthy and Chinese pipa virtuoso Wu Man; and solo projects including the award winning "Cool and Unusual," and "The Bramble Briar." To keep up with Martin's work, visit www.martinsimpson.com.

If you have a firm grasp of reading music and guitar tablature, you may be able to skip this chapter. Scan it to make sure, and if you see any material that seems unfamiliar, study it well. Otherwise, move on to Chapter 2.

 ## MUSIC NOTATION

Learning to read music on the guitar is easy if you apply yourself and have some patience. You may not be able to rip through the Bach lute suites right away, but you'll get the basics covered quickly and, if you stick with it, you'll eventually be reading through more difficult pieces.

PITCH

Notes

Music is written by placing *notes* on a *staff*. Notes appear various ways.

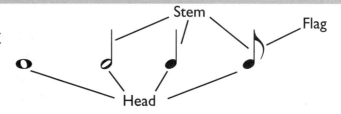

THE STAFF AND CLEF

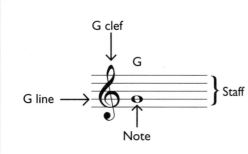

The staff has five lines and four spaces which are read from left to right. At the beginning of the staff is a *clef*. The clef dictates what notes correspond to a particular line or space on the staff. Guitar music is written in *treble clef*, which is sometimes called the *G clef*. The ending curl of the clef encircles the G line on the staff.

Here are the notes on the staff using the G clef:

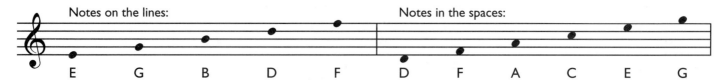

Ledger Lines

The higher a note appears on the staff, the higher it sounds. When a note is too high or too low to be written on the staff, *ledger lines* are used.

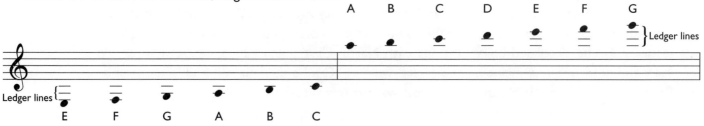

Guitar music is traditionally written one octave higher than it actually sounds. This allows us to write and read music on one clef instead of using two clefs, as with the keyboard instruments.

TIME

Measures and Bar Lines

The staff is divided by vertical lines called *bar lines*. The space between two bar lines is called a *measure*. Measures divide music into groups of *beats*. Beats are equal divisions of time. Beats are the basic pulse behind music. A *double bar* marks the end of a section or example.

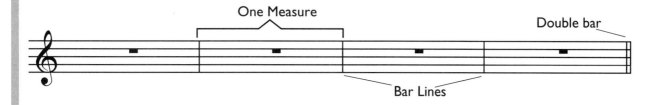

Note Values

The location of a note relative to the staff tells us its *pitch* (how high or low it is). The duration, or value, is indicated by its shape.

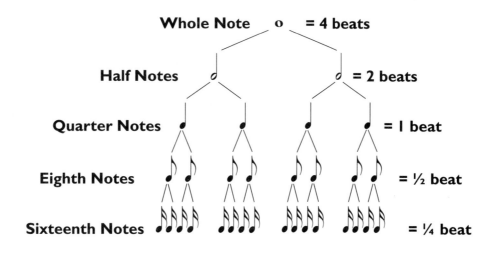

Time Signatures

Every piece of music has numbers at the beginning that tell us how to count time. The top number represents the number of beats per measure. The bottom number represents the type of note receiving one count.

4 ◄ 4 beats per measure
4 ◄ Quarter note ♩ = one beat

3 ◄ 3 beats per measure
4 ◄ Quarter note ♩ = one beat

Sometimes a 𝐂 is written in place of ⁴⁄₄. This is called *common time*.

6 ◄ 6 beats per measure
8 ◄ Eighth note ♪ = one beat

Beaming
Notes that are less than one beat in duration are often beamed together. Notice the counting numbers: Since there are four sixteenth notes in a beat, they are counted "1 e & ah 2 e & ah," and so on.

Beamed eighth notes

1 & 2 & 3 & 4 &

Beamed sixteenth notes

1 e & ah 2 e & ah

Rest Values
Every note value has a corresponding rest. A rest indicates silence. A whole rest indicates four beats of silence, a half rest is two beats of silence, and so on.

➖ = Whole rest, 4 beats

➖ = Half rest, 2 beats

𝄽 = Quarter rest, one beat

𝄾 = Eighth rest, ½ beat

𝄿 = Sixteenth rest, ¼ beat

Ties
When notes are tied, the second note is not struck. Rather, its value is added to that of the first note. So, a half note tied to a quarter note would equal three beats.

🎵‿🎵 = 3 beat

2 + 1

Notice the numbers under the staff in these examples. They indicate how to count. Both of these examples are in ⁴⁄₄ time, so we count four beats in each measure. When there are eighth notes, which are only ½ beat, we count "&" ("and") to show the division of the beats into two parts. When a counting number is in parentheses, a note is being held in a tie rather than struck.

Ties are a convenient way to notate notes that begin off the beat (on an "&").

1   2   &   (3) ↑ &   4

Consecutive eighth notes are *beamed* together. See page 7.

1   &   (2)   &   (3)   &   4

Accidentals
Accidentals arer signs used to raise, lower or return a note top its normal pitch.

♯ = Sharp. Raises the pitch one half step (one fret).

♭ = Flat. Lowers the pitch one half step.

♮ = Natural. Indicates that the note is neither flat or sharp.

Dots

A *dot* increases the duration of a note by one half of its original value. For instance, a half note equals two beats. Half of its value is one beat (a quarter note). So a dotted half note equals three beats (2 + 1 = 3). A dotted half note is equal to a half note tied to a quarter note.

Dotted notes are especially important when the time signature is $\frac{3}{4}$, because the longest note value that will fit in a measure is a dotted half note. Also, dotted notes are very important in $\frac{6}{8}$ time, because not only is a dotted half note the longest possible note value, but a dotted quarter note is exactly half of a measure (counted "1 & ah, 2 & ah").

Triplets

A triplet is a group of three notes that divides a beat (or beats) into three equal parts.

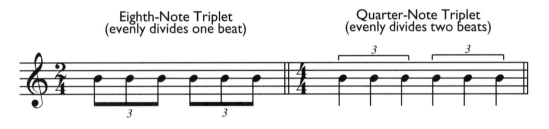

Eighth-Note Triplet
(evenly divides one beat)

Quarter-Note Triplet
(evenly divides two beats)

Go back to the beginning and play these measures one more time.

Play the music between these signs twice.

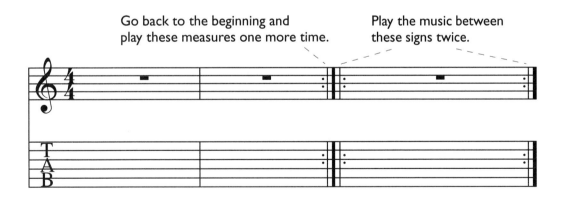

▶ UNDERSTANDING TABLATURE

Tablature is an alternative method of notation used for guitar and other fretted instruments. Forms of it have been in use since before the Renaissance period (1425–1600). When reading tablature, we read fret numbers that tell us exactly where to place our fingers on the neck. Tablature, when combined with standard notation, provides the most complete system for communicating the many possibilities in guitar playing.

In our TAB system, as in most, rhythm is not notated. For that, you will have to refer to the standard notation. Six lines are used to indicate the six strings of the guitar. The top line is the high E string (the string closest to the floor) and the bottom line is the low E string. Numbers are placed on the strings to indicate frets. If there is a "0," play that string open.

Fingerings are sometimes included in TAB. You will find them just under the bottom line. A "1" indicates your left index finger. A "4" indicates your left pinkie.

In the following example, the first note is played with the first finger on the first fret. The next note is played with the second finger on the second fret, the third finger plays the third fret, and the fourth finger plays the fourth fret.

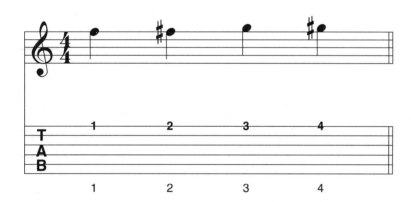

A tie in the music is indicated in TAB by placing the tied note in parentheses.

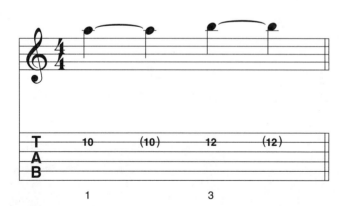

8

Fingerstyle Notation

The standard rule in notation is that notes on the middle line of the staff (or higher) have their stems descending on the left, and lower notes have their stems ascending on the right. This system won't work in fingerstyle, since we are usually writing and playing more than one line at a time. In order to clearly separate the bass line, we must borrow from classical guitar notation: We use descending stems for all notes played by the thumb and ascending stems for all other pitches. This is an easy way to show two or more simultaneous melodic lines. Right-hand fingers are marked with the letters p (thumb), i (index), m (middle) and a (ring).

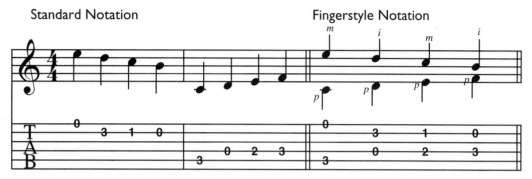

Scale Diagrams

The top line of a scale diagram represents the 1st (highest) string of the guitar; the bottom line the 6th. The vertical lines represent frets, which are numbered below the diagrams.

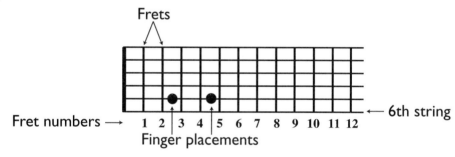

Chord Diagrams

Chord diagrams are similar to scale diagrams, except they are oriented vertically instead of horizontally: Vertical lines represent strings, and horizontal lines represent frets, which are numbered to the left of the diagrams.

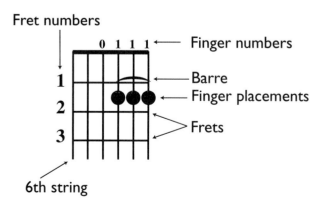

9

In order to understand the discussion of alternate tunings in this book, you'll need to understand some basic music theory. If you are already well acquainted with the major scale, major triads and how chords how are made from scales, you can skip this section and move on to Chapter 3.

▶ HALF STEPS AND WHOLE STEPS

It's very helpful to understand that we can measure the distance between any two notes. The shortest distance between two notes is a *half step*, which is a distance of one fret. For example, the distance from the 1st fret to the 2nd fret is one half step. The distance of two half steps—two frets—is called a *whole step*. For example, the distance from the 1st fret to the 3rd is a whole step.

▶ SCALES

A *scale* is a series of notes arranged in a specific order of whole steps and half steps. The notes of a scale can ascend and/or descend in alphabetical order (the musical alphabet is the first seven letters of the English alphabet, A through G). Each note in the scale is called a *scale degree*. The scale degrees are numbered upward from the lowest note.

MAJOR SCALES

A *major scale* is made up of eight notes with half steps between the 3rd and 4th, and 7th and 8th degrees. The rest are whole steps. The scale takes its name from its lowest note (or 1st degree). The eight notes of the scale span an *octave*, which is the closest distance between any two notes with the same name (12 half steps). The 8th degree is an octave above the 1st degree. Study the placement of whole and half steps represented by the letters "W" and "H" in the following diagram of the C Major scale.

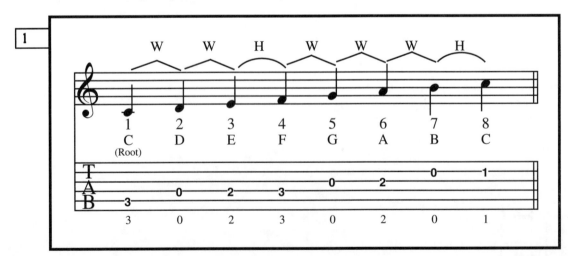

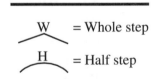

We can also play the same notes in different locations by going vertically across the neck:

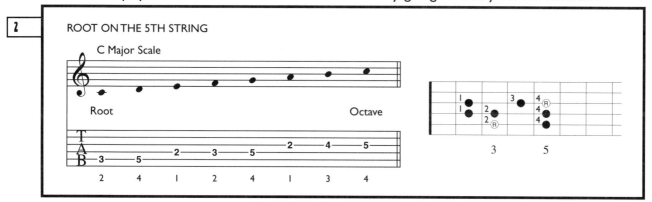

2

ROOT ON THE 5TH STRING

C Major Scale

Root   Octave

The C Major scale is the only one without sharps or flats. If we start on any other *root*, or starting pitch, we will need sharps or flats to complete the formula.

When the root is G, we will need an F♯ to get the whole step between the 6th and 7th notes, since E–F is a half step.

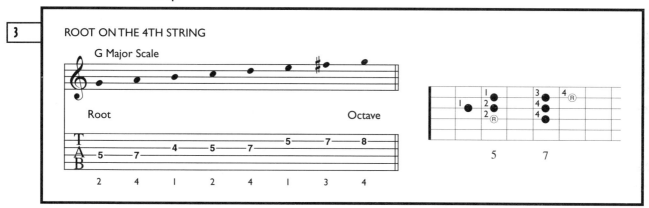

3

ROOT ON THE 4TH STRING

G Major Scale

Root   Octave

▶ CHORDS COME FROM SCALES

The *chords* we use are derived from the major scale. Remember that a chord is three or more notes played together. We build a *triad*, the most basic kind of chord, by simply using every other note in a major scale. For example, here is how we build a C Major chord:

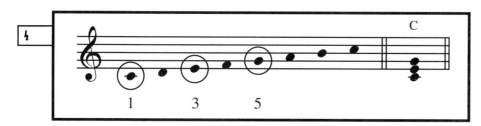

4

Most tunes are based on the relationships between three chords: a chord built on the 1st degree (called I—musicians all over the world use Roman numerals to label chords), a chord built on the 4th degree (called IV) and a chord built on the 5th degree (called V). Here they are in C:

5

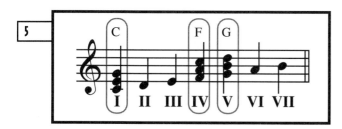

Roman Numeral Review	
I = 1	V = 5
II = 2	VI = 6
III = 3	VII= 7
IV = 4	

This is a major tuning, meaning that all of the strings are tuned to notes from a particular major chord, in this case D Major. There are only three notes in a D Major triad (D–F#–A). These are the root, 3rd and 5th (R–3–5) of the chord. To get the six notes we need on the guitar, the root (D) is tripled, and the 5th is doubled. The 3rd is rarely doubled in a chord voicing.

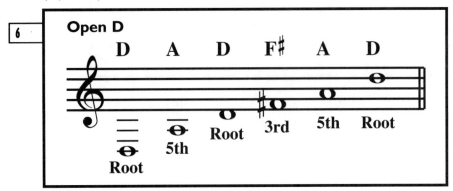

Open D Major has an interesting history. In the 1860s, fingerstyle guitar was a very popular pastime in America. Compositions for fingerstyle guitar would sell very large quantities in sheet music, and one such composition, called *Sebastopol*, was one of the greatest hits of the time. It was composed in Open D Major tuning. It very rapidly passed out of the parlors in which fingerstyle guitar was played and became a standard. In the southern United States, there are still people who refer to this tuning as "Vestapol" tuning, which is a shortening of the word Sebastopol.

If you have a guitar like mine, with a long scale and medium-gauge strings, you will always want to tune your instrument *down* to these tunings. But, of course, if we put a barre or capo anywhere on the fretboard, we'll get the same intervals and the same relationships between the strings. By the same logic, if you have a short-scale guitar with light strings, or an electric guitar, rather than tune down to Open D, you might want to tune up to Open E. That would give you E–B–E–G#–B–E. The intervals between the strings are the same as in Open D, but the pitches are different.

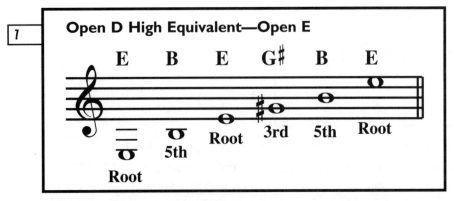

In old recordings by Robert Johnson, some of the slide playing is in this Open E tuning—it's very intense and very bright. Because of the relationships between the intervals, open tunings will dictate what is possible to play. Open D tuning is a perfect place to start experimenting with bottleneck (slide) because you have the root–5th–root relationships in the bass, and a full octave of melody strings on the top. The R–5–R in the bass allows for lots of playing without fretted bass notes, and the full octave of melody strings on the treble side leaves lots of room for melodic playing.

R = Root

▶ TUNING TO OPEN D

We will tune to Open D from standard tuning, which is as follows:

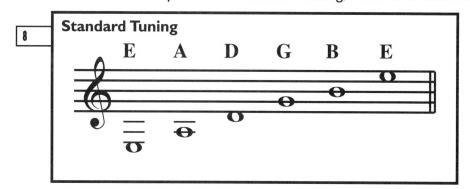

8

Notice that with the 5th and 4th strings of standard tuning, we already have the 5th and the root of the D Major chord. First, we will lower the 6th string from E to D. You can match the open 4th string to the harmonic at the 12th fret of the 6th string. This gives us the R–5–R relationship on the 6th, 5th and 4th strings. This is a *power chord*. Those of you who play rock'n'roll guitar now have an instant power chord on your bass strings. All it takes is one finger and you can write heavy metal songs—a wonderful concept!

9 Step 1

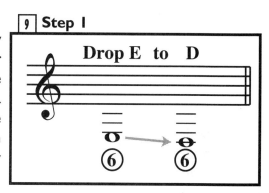

Next, drop the 1st string E down a whole step to D. Just match the 1st string to the harmonic at the 12th fret of the 4th string. **As you re-tune, be aware that you're dropping notes a long way in pitch. The general pitch of the guitar *may* rise a little, and you will have to keep adjusting as you re-tune each string.** So, now we have R–5–R in the bass plus a root on the top string.

10 Step 2

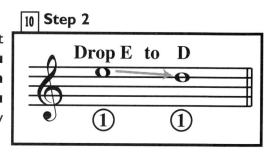

What we're going to do next is lower the 2nd string B until it sounds an octave above the 5th string A. Match it to the 5th string harmonic at the 12th fret. So, we now have R–5–R in the bass and 5–R on the top two strings.

11 Step 3

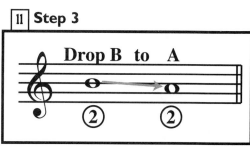

All that is left for us to change is the 3rd string. We're going to drop this one half step to F♯, which is the major 3rd of the chord. Match the 3rd string to the 4th fret of the 4th string.

12 Step 4

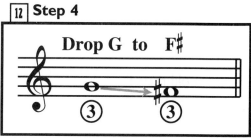

The intervals—and this is the way I want you to think of this tuning and all the other tunings—are as follows: root, 5th, root, 3rd, 5th, root: R–5–R–3–5–R.

► BARRE CHORDS IN OPEN D

Anywhere we put a full barre chord on the fretboard is going to give us a major chord. So we can play I, IV and V as follows:

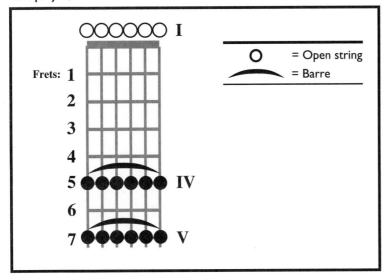

Roman Numeral Review	
I = 1	V = 5
II = 2	VI = 6
III = 3	VII= 7
IV = 4	

► A SIMPLE IV CHORD

If you listen to the early recordings of Joni Mitchell and many other guitarists who use open tunings, you're going to hear this movement from the open strings to a IV chord:

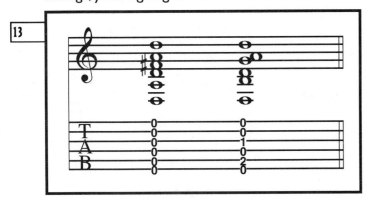

This is the simplest form of a IV chord triad in Open D:

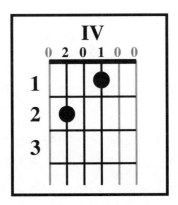

Remember, a chord can be built on each note in the major scale (see page 11), and if you're singing a simple, traditional song in a major key, you would most likely be using the I chord, the IV chord and the V chord. Since this is the simplest form of a IV chord triad, this shape is very important; we're going to be seeing it again and again.

If I put a barre at the 5th fret and add this simple IV-chord shape on top of it, you hear the same chord sound at a different pitch.

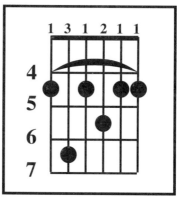

This shape can also be moved up the neck without a barre, combined with the open strings of Open D to create some beautiful sounds.

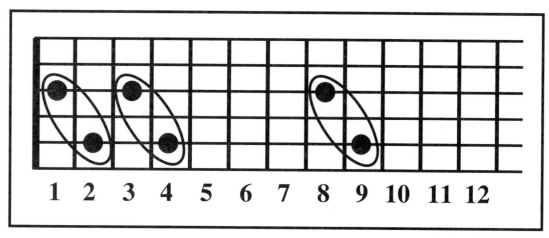

Using this shape and another parallel shape at the 5th, 7th, 10th and 12th frets, we can create a beautiful harmonization of the D Major scale.

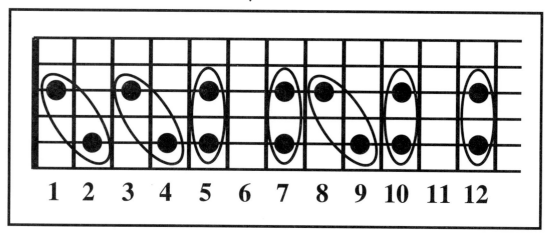

Like Open D tuning, Open G Major also has a considerable history in America, and it is also a tuning which has come to be known by a common name. In the 1860s or so, there was a great fingerstyle guitar hit called *Spanish Fandango*, which was composed in Open G tuning. This became very widespread and again, in the southern United States, you still find older players who refer to Open G tuning as "Spanish Tuning" because of *Spanish Fandango*. The tune *Spanish Fandango* itself is still popular and can be found in several forms, including the rather delightfully corrupted *Spanish Flangdang* (as recorded by players such as Mississippi John Hurt and Elizabeth Cotten).

▶ TUNING TO OPEN G FROM OPEN D

We're now going to retune from Open D to Open G tuning. And always, the first thing to do in retuning is to establish which notes will be common to both tunings. Here is a reminder of Open D:

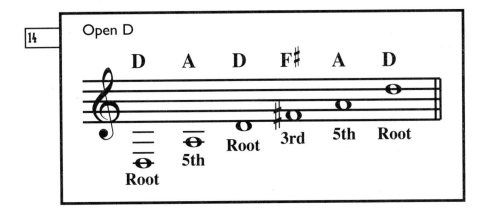

The three Ds shown below are going to stay right where they are. They're going to cease to be the root of the D Major chord and become the 5th of the G Major chord.

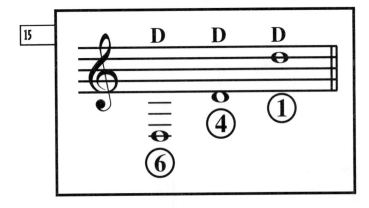

We have no Gs in Open D, so we must create them for Open G tuning. The 5th fret of the 4th string is G, so we can match the 3rd-string F♯ to it in order to tune up one half step to G.

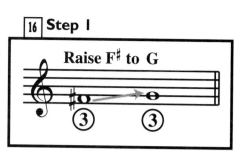

Now, drop the 5th-string A one whole step to G, an octave below the 3rd string. You can match the harmonic at the 12th fret of the 5th string to the open 3rd string. We now have 5–R–5–R on the 6th, 5th, 4th and 3rd strings.

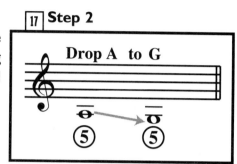

We need to adjust the 2nd-string A to fit into our G Major triad scheme. We will make it a B by matching it to the 3rd string at the 4th fret.

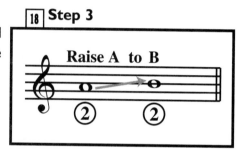

Here are the notes of Open G Major tuning:

Notice the intervals: 5–R–5–R–3–5.

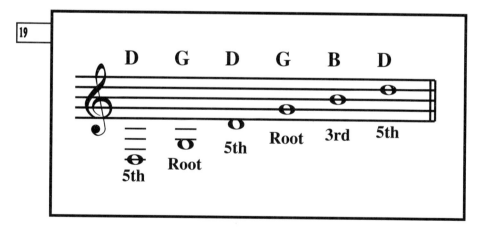

▶ THE SIMPLE IV CHORD IN OPEN G

In Open D tuning, we had R–5–R on the bottom strings. We now have moved that over to the next set of strings—the 5th, 4th and 3rd—and above the R–5–R we have a major 3rd (3) and another 5th (5) on the 2nd and 1st strings, respectively.

If you look at the diagram below, you will see that the Open G tuning sits underneath Open D with the 6th string moved over. And you will see that the 6th string interval is now the 5th instead of the root. It is very important to keep track of how the R–5–R pattern is situated in each tuning.

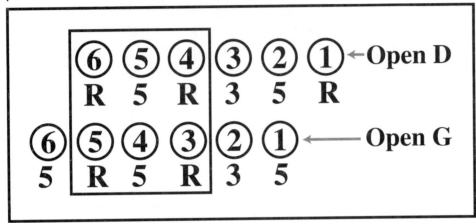

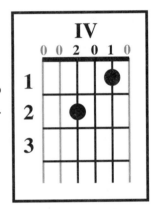

This means that when we go to play our simple IV chord position, we're going to use exactly the same shape because we're working on exactly the same intervals. Everything is just moved over one string towards the treble.

Joni Mitchell used this I to IV shape as a compositional element in many of her early songs, and you can hear the exact same thing in the work of The Rolling Stones' Keith Richards. He plays a Telecaster low on his right hip and hits the guitar at arm's length from above. He takes the 6th string off and plays with the remaining five strings in Open G tuning. So the first interval he hits is a 5th (G to D). Many of The Rolling Stones' signature hits are played in this tuning.

Here is the I to IV move we saw on page 14, now in Open G and moved over one string set.

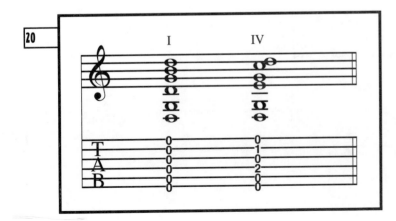

We've established that we have exactly the same intervals as Open D Major. But if we stop for a minute and examine the relationship of this tuning to standard tuning, we'll find something very interesting and informative.

The open 4th, 3rd and 2nd strings—D, G, B—which are the 5th, root and major 3rd of this tuning, are common to Open G and standard tunings. We have these same intervals in Open D tuning (the 5th, 4th and 3rd strings).

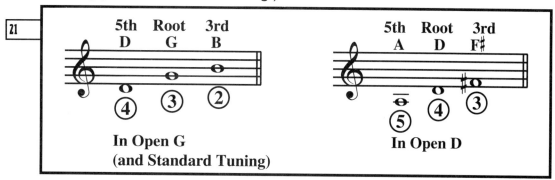

We can remind ourselves of that by just thinking about the relationship between the easy IV triads in Open D and Open G. What we can learn from these relationships—between standard, Open D and Open G tunings—is very helpful and very useful: Anything that works in standard tuning or Open D on these three strings—5–R–3—will work in Open G tuning.

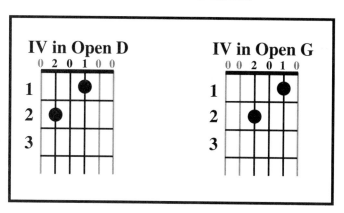

▶ THE G MAJOR SCALE

Let's pause for a minute and look at the R–5–R area of this tuning:

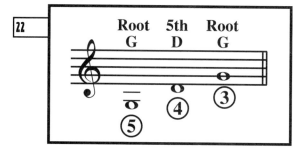

When we play in standard tuning, we're constantly having to think about chord shapes and relationships, which vary across the fingerboard. In this tuning, and in all the major open tunings, you have much less information to deal with, and it's very simple to learn to play scales in this R–5–R area.

Bass lines are very easy to find using this scale.

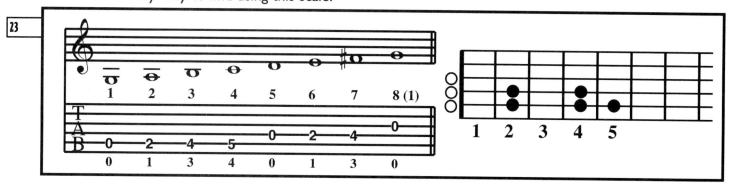

▶ SOME OTHER CHORDS IN OPEN G

Let's look at some chord shapes that we're very familiar with in standard tuning.

C

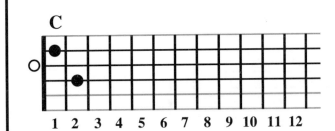

C

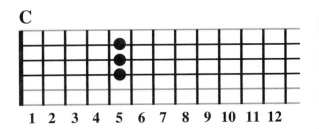

D7

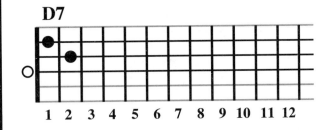

D

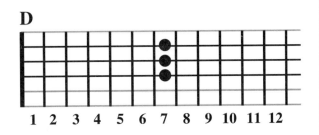

E Minor

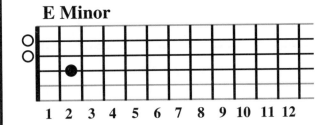

E Minor

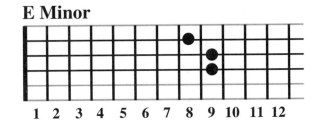

A Minor

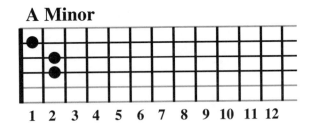

F

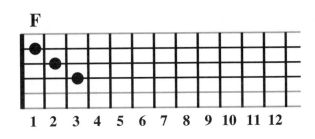

B Minor

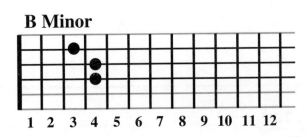

All these little shapes are *moveable*—they can be played in any position on the fretboard. So let's play a harmonized major scale using these familiar shapes: G, A Minor, B Minor, C, D, E Minor and D. You can go ahead and strum all of the other, open strings for a beautiful effect.

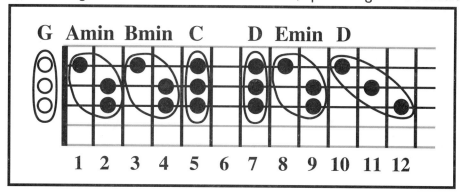

Below is a "hollowed-out" version of the same ascending harmonization. Again, including the open strings works well.

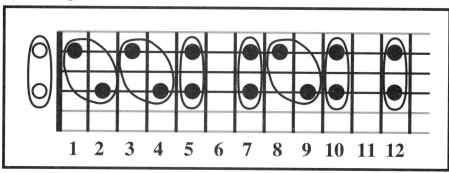

Here's another form using 3rds:

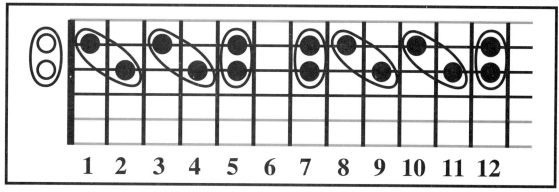

In this tuning, as in all the major tunings, we have a lot of parallel possibilities so we can also play the lower notes in the 3rds an octave below.

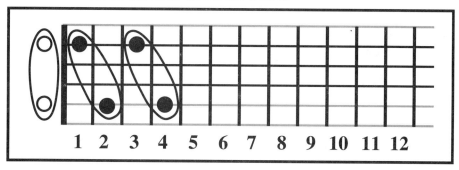

Take some time to look at the chord diagrams and find your way around the fingerboard using those chords. You'll find many ideas will come to mind.

What we're going to do now is move from Open G to Open C, which is the final major tuning in this book. Open C tuning extends the range of the guitar on the bass side, because we drop the 6th string a very long way.

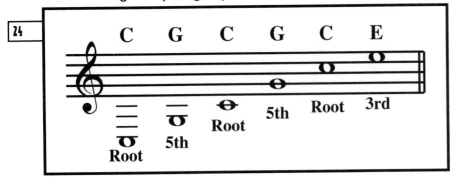

In my introduction to Open D tuning (page 12), I talked about the high equivalent, which was Open E. Open G (page 16) also has a high equivalent, which is Open A—just raise the pitch of each string by one whole step. Open C also has its high equivalent, which shows the importance of the relationships between these tunings, because the high equivalent of Open C is Open D. The notes are D–A–D–A–D–F♯.

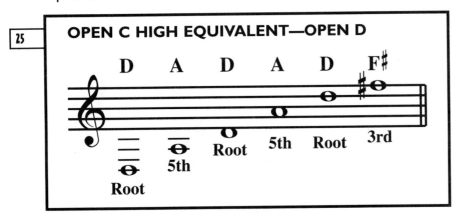

We ordinarily choose to tune strings downward. In this tuning, the 3rd and 1st strings are tuned upward. This is unusual and about as far up as you want to go.

If you think just for a moment in terms of notes rather than intervals, you can see that the top four strings are now effectively an octave above the bottom four strings in Open D (page 12).

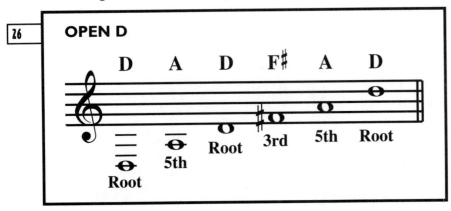

Remember to think about the intervals because when we go to play our easy IV chord, it's exactly the same shape as it has been for Open D and Open G tunings (shown on page 24). And the shapes all the moveable triads remain the same although they are moved over one set of strings.

TUNING TO OPEN C FROM OPEN G

Let's start by establishing what remains the same as we tune from Open G to Open C. The G notes on the open 5th and 3rd strings are common to the two tunings. They were roots in Open G but will become the 5th in Open C.

We will begin by raising the 2nd string one half step from its current B to C. Match the open 2nd string to the 3rd string, 5th fret. This is one of only two occurences of tuning a string upward to create one of these low, altered tunings.

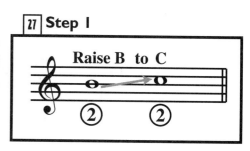

Drop the 4th-string D note one whole step to C, an octave below the 2nd-string C. You can match the 12th fret harmonic of the 4th string to the open 2nd string. Now, on the 4th, 3rd and 2nd strings, we have this much of the tuning working for us: R–5–R.

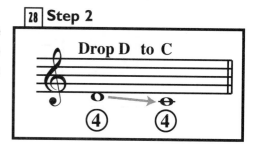

We're going to drop the 6th string D down one whole step to low C, an octave below the 4th string. Match the 12th fret harmonic on the 6th string to the open 4th string. This tuning is unique in that it now gives us, from bass to treble, R–5–R–5–R.

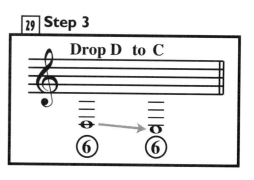

We raise the 1st string one whole step from its current position at D to E. Match the open 1st string to the 4th fret of the 2nd string. This is the second of two times that we raise a string for this kind of tuning.

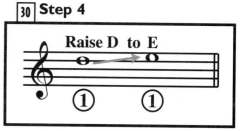

Although we have tuned it up from Open G tuning, the only string that's raised above standard tuning is the 2nd string.

COMPARING OPEN C, OPEN G AND OPEN D

If we examine this tuning and look at the diagram below, you'll see that what we've done is move further to the left of our original tuning. Again we have a root on the 6th string, as we did in Open D. So we have R–5–R, which is where we started, but we also have R–5–R again on the 4th, 3rd and 2nd strings, and a 3rd above that.

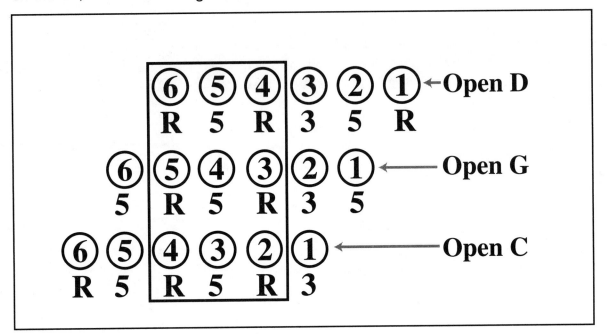

THE SIMPLE IV CHORD IN OPEN C

To play the simple form of the IV chord in Open C, we find it on the top four strings.

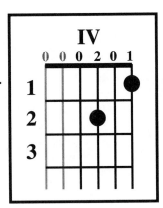

Here is the Open C version of the familiar open-tuning move between I and IV:

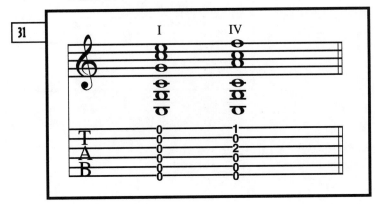

Notice that as we have moved from right to left in the diagram on page 24, the easy IV chord has moved from lower to higher strings (from left to right in the chord diagrams). The most important thing, though, is that its shape remains unchanged.

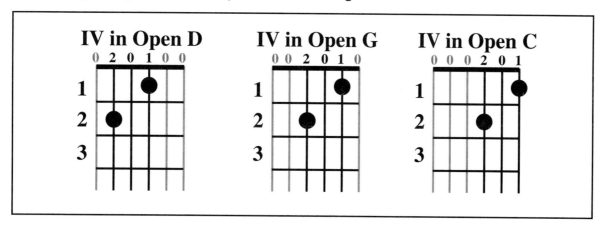

SOME OTHER USEFUL CHORDS

As you learn these chords, remember that they can be applied to Open G by moving them to the next lower set of strings and adapting as needed. You can also move them over once more to use them in Open D.

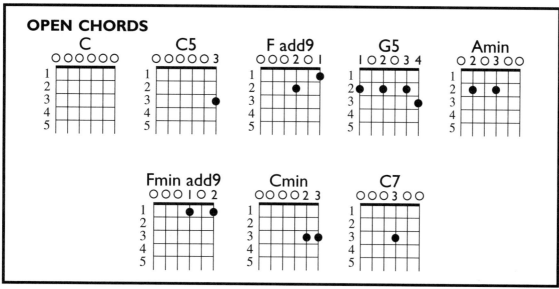

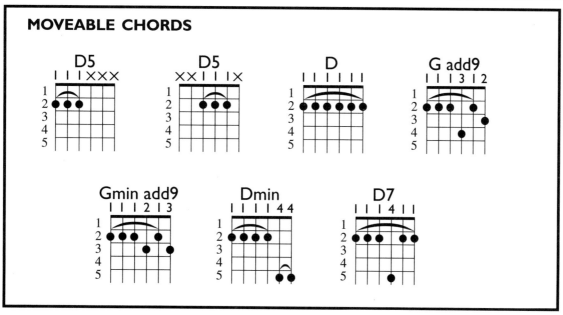

Unlike the tunings we have investigated so far, DADGAD is not a major tuning, which means it is not strictly an open tuning. Rather, it is generally referred to as an alternate tuning. DADGAD is what we call a *modal tuning*—since it doesn't dictate major or minor—and it's wonderful for playing all different kinds of world music.

The history of DADGAD is fascinating. In the early 1960s, a very well-known and influential English guitar player, Davy Graham, took the "hippie trail" to North Africa, where he experimented with his consciousness and met and played with Moroccan musicians. He discovered that he wasn't able to play with North African musicians in standard tuning. He had a very good background in traditional American and British music, and probably already used Open D tuning to play the music of Blind Willie Johnson and other gospel and blues pieces. At some point he found himself almost midway between standard tuning and Open D: from the 6th string to the 1st, D–A–D–G–A–D, which is sort of a Dsus4 tuning. Since then, this tuning has become extremely well known simply as DADGAD. (It is also interesting to note that there is a five-string banjo tuning called Gsus4 that is very similar, see page 30).

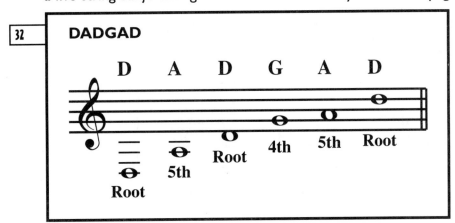

▶ TUNING TO DADGAD FROM OPEN D

We're going to get to DADGAD from its closest related tuning, Open D 9 (see page 12).

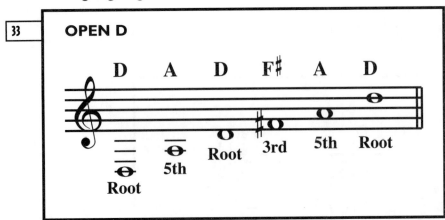

From Open D, we simply return the 3rd string from F♯ back to G. You can match it to the G at the 5th fret of the 4th string.

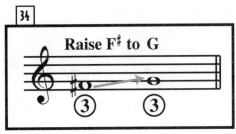

Now we have, from the 6th string to the 1st, R–5–R–4–5–R.

Just in case you are worried that, since we have moved away from a straight, major chord open tuning, we have to completely rethink everything, remember what we've got here: we have R–5–R on the three lowest strings, just as in Open D and Open C. We already know how to play scales with this configuration of intervals.

▶THE MIXOLYDIAN MODE

The *Mixolydian mode* is a major scale with a ♭7 (the 7th degree is lowered one half step from its position in the major scale).

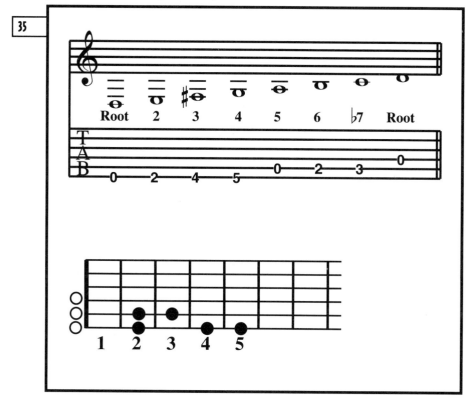

A lot of traditional music from around the world is played with the Mixolydian scale—Irish music, "old-timey" music, and so on—and it works beautifully in this tuning.

►CHORDS IN DADGAD

Let's look and see if we can find something in DADGAD that's common with a more familiar tuning. Stepping aside from the concept of how the intervals in open tunings relate, what we have here on the 5th, 4th and 3rd strings is a big chunk of standard tuning.

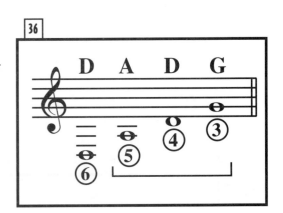

This means that anything we can do on those three strings in standard tuning, we can do where appropriate in DADGAD. So, we can play a C Major triad, with the bottom part of the familiar chord shape.

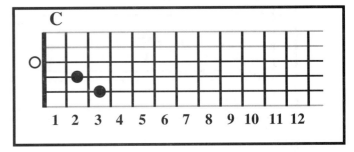

We can do the same with E Minor.

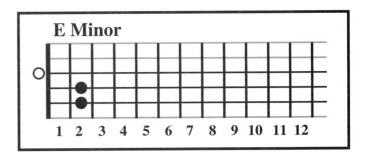

Here are a few more familiar shapes, borrowed from standard tuning, that we can use in DADGAD.

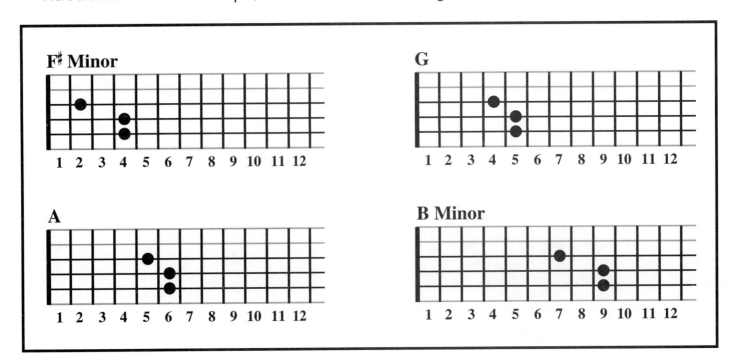

28

In addition, there are some partial chord forms, using just a few strings.

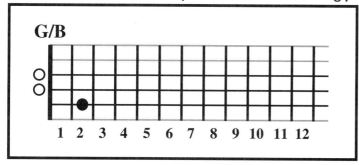

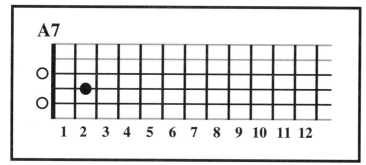

And if we include other open strings, we can play beautiful-sounding chords very simply:

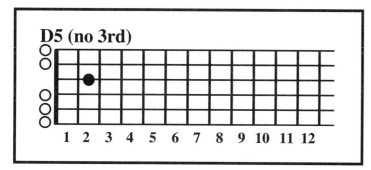

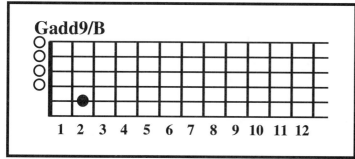

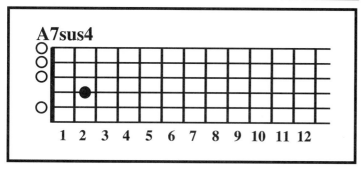

The simplicity of those chords, plus the accessibility of the bass—bass lines are so easy to play in this tuning—make DADGAD extraordinarily accessible. It is no wonder that it spread more rapidly than any other tuning I can think of, and is in very wide usage.

Open Gsus4 tuning has a great deal of precedent in traditional music. It is used in American "old-timey" music, and the banjo is often tuned this way. Using this tuning, you can play banjo tunes on the guitar exactly as you would play them on the banjo. If you listen to the great old-timey banjo players such as Clarence Ashley, you'll hear this tuning in use all the time. You may also notice that this sound is very reminiscent of the blues. Suspended 4th tunings are great blues tunings. They are also wonderful for playing Irish airs, for accompanying songs, and I'm sure for a whole lot of things that I haven't even thought of yet.

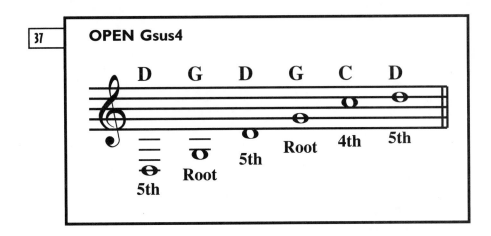

▶ TUNING TO OPEN Gsus4

We're always trying to relate one thing to another, and if you look at the chart on the right, you can see that all we had to do was raise the 3rd of Open D to create DADGAD, another suspended 4th tuning.

We can do exactly the same thing with Open G—

just raise the 3rd to create Gsus4.

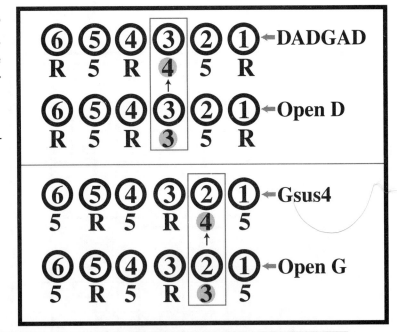

So, to get into Gsus4 from Open G tuning (page 16), ... do this:

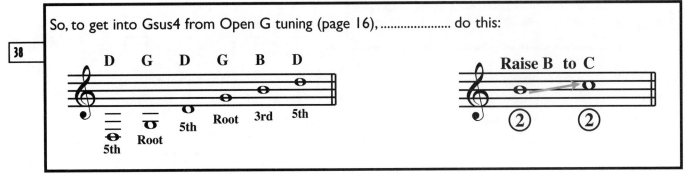

▶OPEN Gsus4 COMPARED TO DADGAD AND STANDARD—SIMPLE CHORDS

What makes suspended-4th modal tunings such as DADGAD and Gsus4 so useful and so attractive is that you can move easily and seamlessly from major sounds to minor sounds, from major 7 to minor 7♭5. But let's just remind ourselves that we are sharing intervals between DADGAD and Gsus4. Gsus4 is one string to the left of DADGAD in the chart below, meaning that chord shapes are now moved over to the next higher set of strings. Compare the chords on page 28 to those at the bottom of this page.

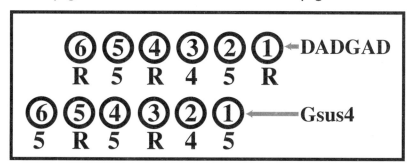

Gsus4 also shares two open strings with standard tuning.

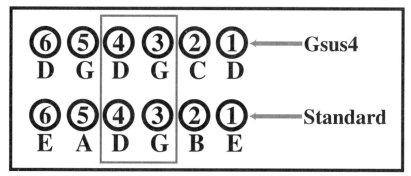

We can also share the chord shapes—the triads—from standard tuning. This is the ♭VII triad, F Major in Gsus4, which will be familiar to you.

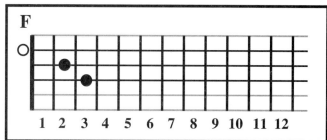

Here are some more chord forms in Gsus4 which, because of the close relationship between this tuning and both DADGAD and standard tunings, will all be somewhat familiar:

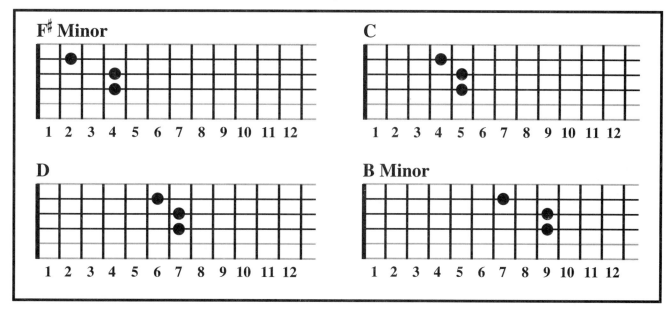

For this tuning, I prefer slightly lighter strings and play with a slightly different tone and approach. Since this is a minor tuning, it has a minor 3rd ($\flat$3). A great way to train your ear to hear these different intervals is to associate the feelings that they might give you. If we think of the major tunings—Open D, Open G and Open C, which have major 3rds—as being smiley, happy-sounding tunings, by comparison, D Minor has a sad sound. This is because of the minor 3rd.

▶ TUNING TO OPEN D MINOR

The best route to D Minor tuning is through Open D, so we will start from that tuning (page 12). Here it is:

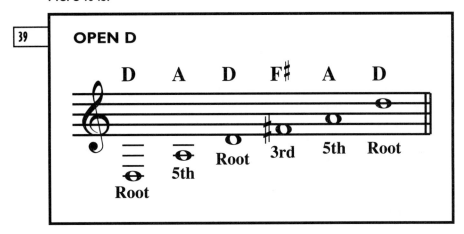

First, let's take the major 3rd and drop it by a half step. You can tune the open 3rd string to the 3rd fret of the 4th string, which is F$\natural$.

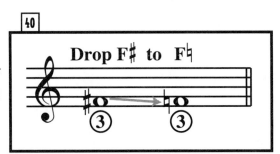

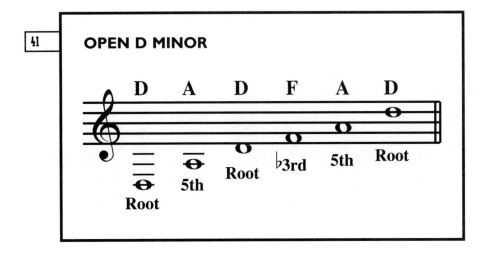

The open minor tuning dictates a mood immediately. There's an ambiance to that minor 3rd. We can do exactly the same thing in Open G or Open C. Take those major 3rds, drop them a half step, and we will have very accessible minor tunings.

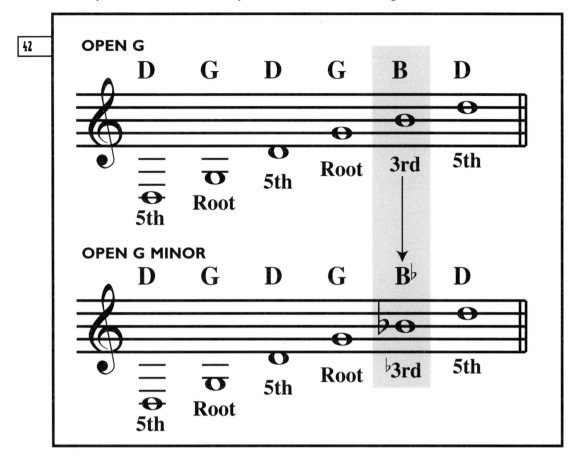

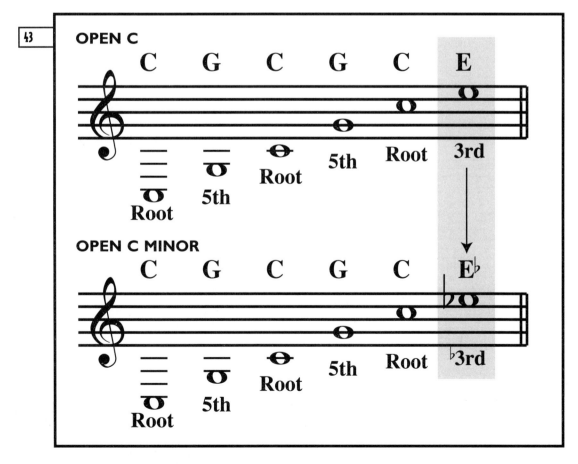

▶COMPARING OPEN D MINOR TO STANDARD TUNING

In D Minor tuning, there's a very interesting parallel. The intervals between the top three strings should be very familiar. These bare the same relationship to each other as the top three strings in standard tuning, which outline an E Minor triad.

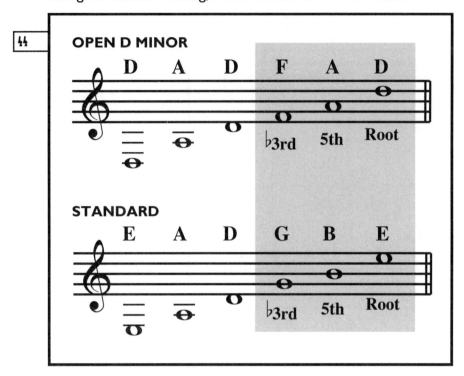

Blues players took notice of this and used it to great effect. You can easily play many familiar scales on the top three strings in D Minor tuning, including blues scales. Replacing the major 3rd (with the index finger) is easy, and is a very typical blues move.

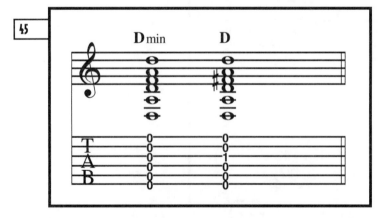

This particular kind of little flutter between the minor 3rd and the major 3rd is a very characteristic sound of the minor tuning. Listen to Skip James. He used this tuning a great deal and moved in and out of major and minor, which achieved very interesting harmonizations.

Csus2, which some people like to call Cadd9, is similar to DADGAD and Gsus4 in that it is neither major or minor. It is another modal tuning which is very useful and one of my particular favorites.

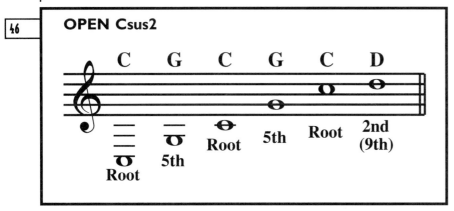

46

OPEN Csus2

C   G   C   G   C   D

Root   5th   Root   5th   Root   2nd (9th)

This is a most unusual tuning. There's a great precedent for it. The old-timey banjo tuning, Double C, is in fact exactly this, and claw-hammer banjo players play fiddle tunes and song accompaniments in this tuning. I find it tremendously useful because one can exploit the intervals between the root and 5th on the 6th through 2nd strings, and there are lots of opportunities for little, partial chords in different octaves. The open strings, and the extended range of the tuning—going as low as C, a major 3rd below the normal low E—provide a wonderful palette of colors to work with. And the D on the 1st string is harmonically sympathetic to almost anything we might do. It is also very easy to play fuller chords. Try experimenting with some of the chords from Open C tuning on page 25. Where possible, just drop the notes on the 1st string one whole step (two frets).

▶ TUNING TO OPEN Csus2

The best route to Csus2 is through Open C tuning (page 22).

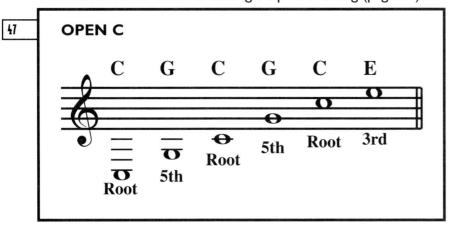

47

OPEN C

C   G   C   G   C   E

Root   5th   Root   5th   Root   3rd

Take the major 3rd on the 1st string (E) and drop it a whole step to D. You can match the 1st string to the D on the 2nd fret of the 2nd string.

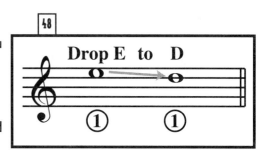

48

Drop E to D

①   ①

So we now have this very close interval between the root on the 2nd string and 2nd on the adjacent 1st string. From bass to treble, we have R–5–R–5–R–2.

IN CONCLUSION

We have covered a huge amount of information. If you examine it carefully, however, it is easy to understand. In all of these tunings, we have R–5–R–5–R and another interval. Where the other interval lies, be it a major 3rd, a 4th, a minor 3rd or a 2nd, will depend on the initial family that you come from. So if it's in D Major, generally speaking, you're going to have that different interval on the 3rd string. In G, it's going to be the 2nd string. In C, it's going to be the 1st string.

That's the basic rule, if you can call it a rule, of this entire system. R–5–R is common to all of these tunings. Then you will have another root and 5th above or below that and one other interval.

There are other alterations we can make. It's possible, for example, to make a suspended 4th tuning out of Open C.

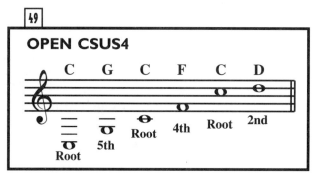

I do that regularly. I alter the 5th (G) on the 3rd string by lowering it a whole step and that gives me what at first might seem a little bewildering set of intervals: R–5–R–4–R–2.

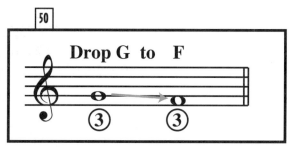

I've asked you to think in terms of intervals all the time. Think now about what we have here: R–5–R–4. Those are the same intervals as the bottom four strings of DADGAD. Above it, instead of having 5–R, we have R–2. So we can treat the bottom four strings as if we were playing in DADGAD, and above them have some very interesting, close harmonies.

There are many, many open tunings out there, but if you approach the whole idea from this point of view—that there's a great deal of logic and some very clear theory involved in your work with these tunings—I think you'll have a very good time exploring. Don't be afraid to get lost! Getting lost is sometimes the best thing that you can do, because you learn so much as you find your way back.

I hope this has been useful and helpful. It really is a road map, so see how far it can take you.

Editor's Note
The rest of the book is a set of ten different pieces, all of which are in alternate tunings (some that are covered in this book and some that are not). They are offered for your enjoyment and as examples of the many possibilities these tunings present. Two of them, *Raglan Road* and *James Connolly* (mistakenly called *The Plains of Waterloo* in the video) are performed on the DVD that is included with this book. The complete lyrics to *The Bramble Briar* and *Polly on the Shore* are printed on pages 60 and 61 respectively. Following the pieces and lyrics is a brief summary of the tunings found in this book.

RAGLAN ROAD—Csus2 (page 35)

Traditional
arr. Martin Simpson

Capo 2

Tune to:
D
C
G
C
G
C

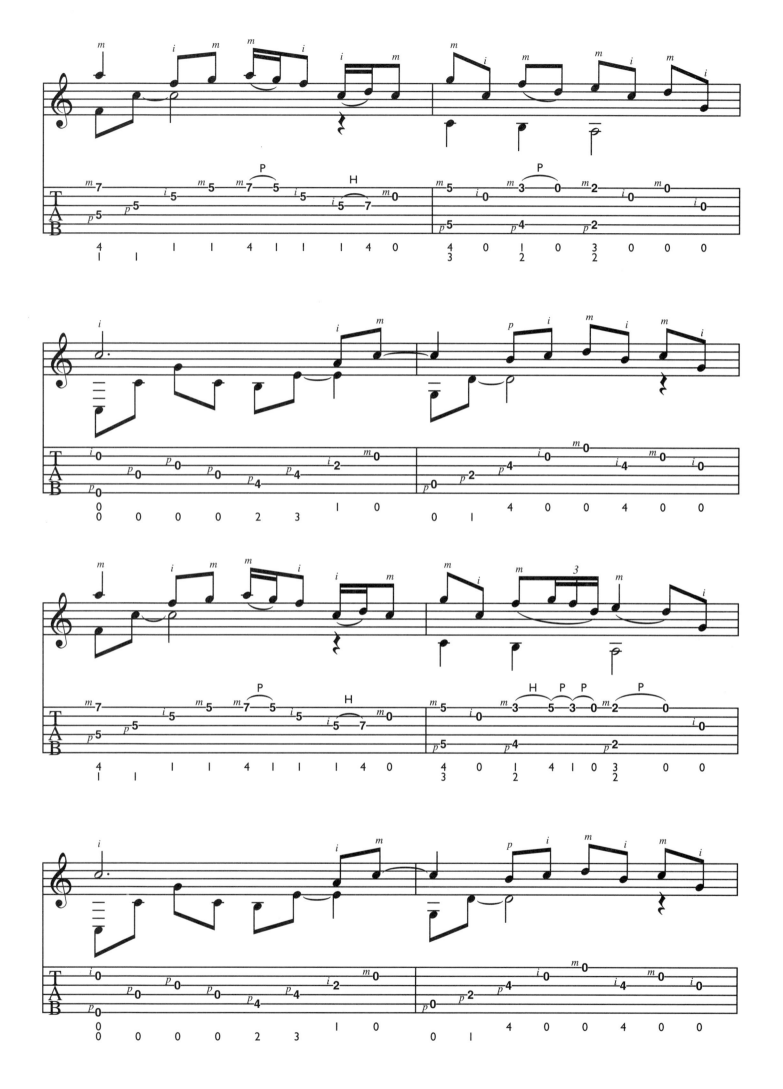

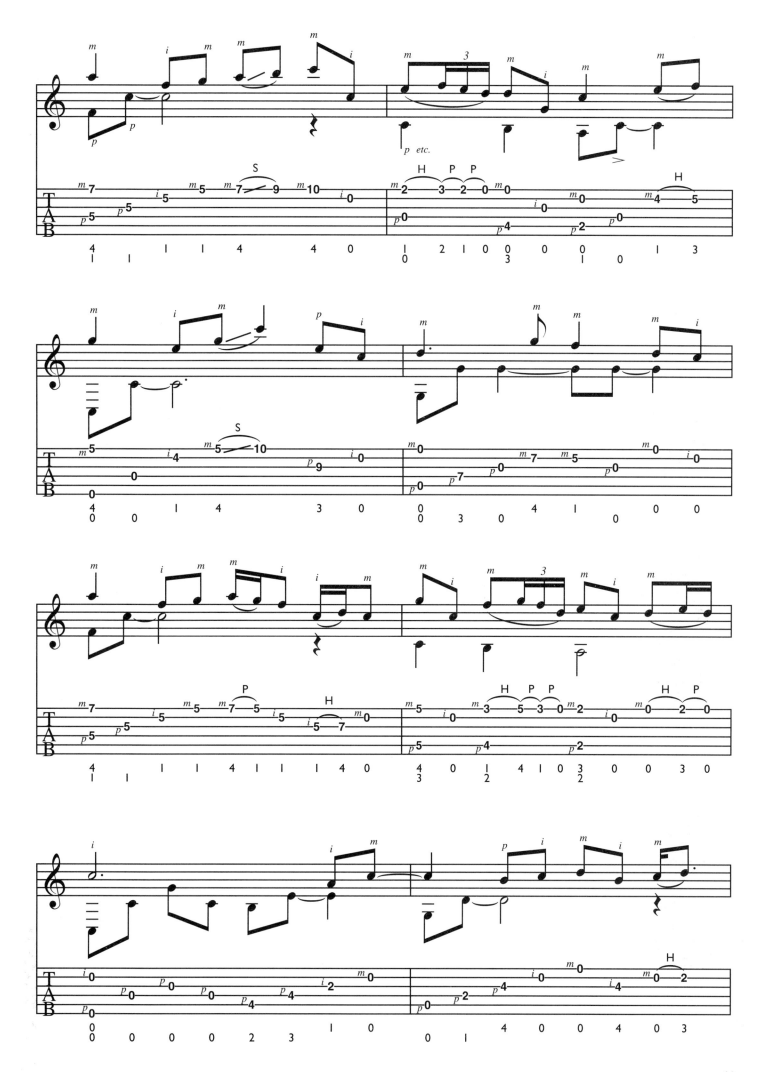

JAMES CONNOLLY–Csus2 (page 35)

Traditional
arr. Martin Simpson

Tune to:

D
C
G
C
G
C

All fretted notes with slide. Use vibrato throughout

THE FLOWER OF SWEET ERIN THE GREEN—Gsus4 (page 30)

Traditional
arr. Martin Simpson

Tune to:
D
C
G
G
D

45

GARRYOWEN–DADGAD (page 26)

Traditional
arr. Martin Simpson

Slow and free

Tune to:
DADGAD

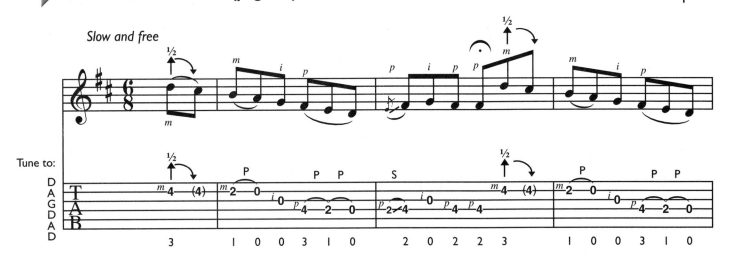

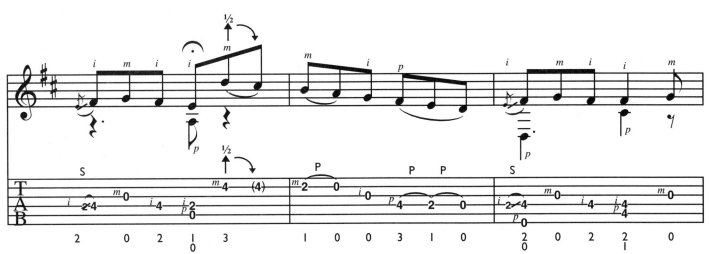

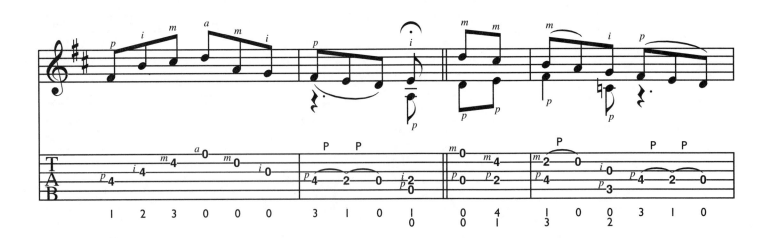

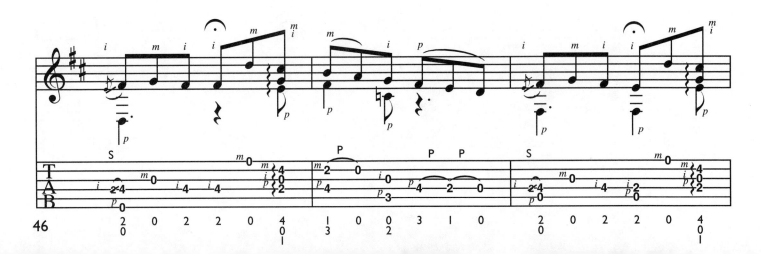

47

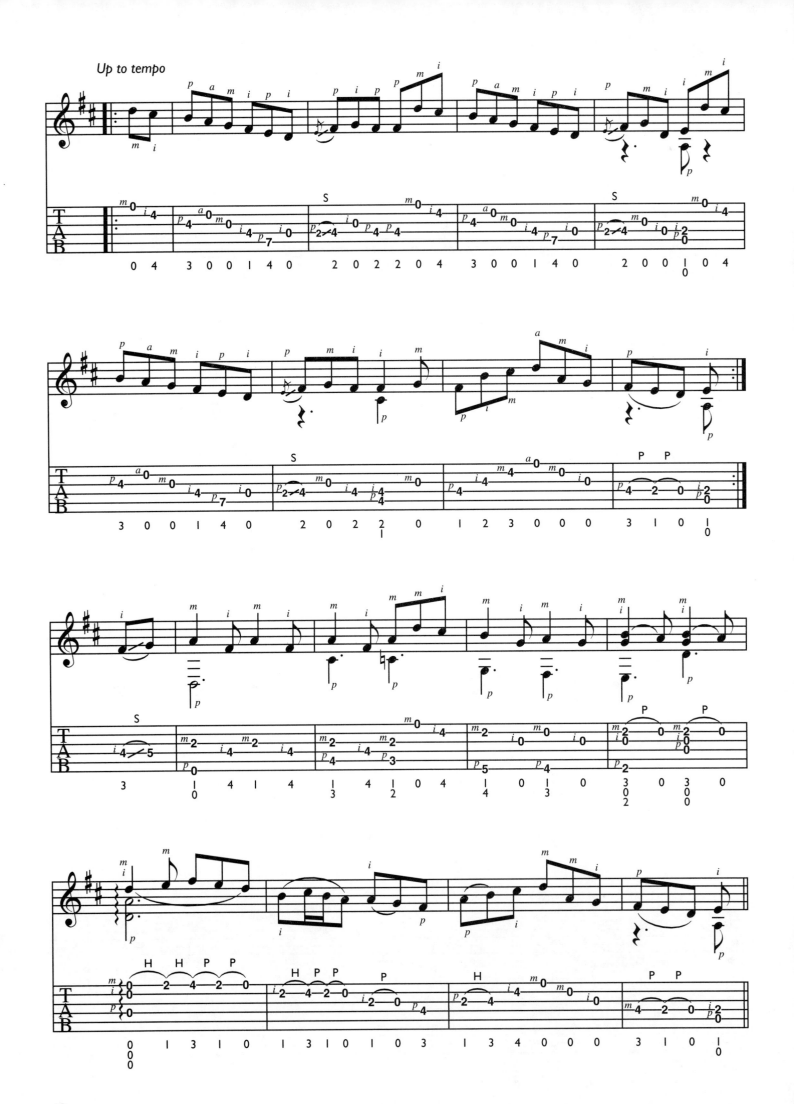

O JERUSALEM—OPEN G (page 16)

Traditional
arr. Martin Simpson

Capo 3

Tune to:
D
B
G
D
G
D

49

THE PLAINS OF WATERLOO—Gsus2 (page 35)

Traditional
arr. Martin Simpson

Tune to:

D
A
G
D
G
D

THE BRAMBLE BRIAR–DADGAD (page 26)

The complete lyrics are printed on page 60.

Verses 1-2

1. In Bru-ton Town there lived a farm-er who had two sons and a daugh-ter dear, By day and night they were con-triv-ing to fill their pa-rents' heart with fear. 2. He mind to wed. I'll put an end to all their court-ship, I'll

1.

2.

send him si - lent to his grave.

asked him to go out a - hunt - ing, with - out an - y fear or

Verses 3–6, 7–10, 11–12

54

strife, And these two bold and wick-ed vil-lains, they took a - way this

D.S. after vs. 6, 10
D.S. al Coda after v.12

Coda

young man's life. 4. And

Traditional
arr. Martin Simpson

This tuning is the same as Gsus4 (page 30), but the 6th string is one whole step lower (C instead of D).

The complete lyrics are printed on page 61.

board a man-of-war I did go. When I was pressed by a

sea cap-tain And on board a man-of-war I did go.

D.S. after v.4
Continue after v.7

Ending

▶ LYRICS—THE BRAMBLE BRIAR

INTRO

1.   In Bruton Town there lived a farmer who had two sons and a daughter dear,
By day and night they were contriving to fill their parents' heart with fear.

2.   He told his secrets to no other, unto his brother this he said,
I think our servant courts our sister, I think they has a great mind to wed.
I'll put an end to all their courtship, I'll send him silent to his grave.

BREAK

3   They asked him to go out a-hunting, without any fear or strife,
And these two bold and wicked villains, they took away this young man's life.

4.   And in the ditch there was no water, where only bush and briars grew,
They could not hide the blood of slaughter, so in the ditch his body they threw.

5.   When they returned home from hunting, she's asking for her serving man,
I ask because I see you whisper, brothers, tell me if you can.

6.   Oh sister, sister, you do offend me, because you so examine me,
We lost him where we've been a-hunting, no more of him we could not see.

BREAK

7   As she lay dreaming on her pillow, she thought she saw her heart's delight
By her bedside as she lay weeping; he was dressed all in his bloody coat.

8.   Don't weep for me my dearest jewel, don't weep for me, nor care nor pine,
For your two brothers killed me cruel, in such a place you may me find.

9.   She early rose the very next morning, with a heavy sigh and a bitter groan,
The only love that she admired, she found in the ditch where he was thrown.

10.   The blood upon his lips was drying, her tears were salt as any brine,
She sometimes kissed him, sometimes crying, Here lies the dearest friend of mine.

BREAK

11.   Three days and nights she did sit by him, till her poor heart was filled with woe,
And cruel hunger crept upon her, and home she was obliged to go.

12.   Sister, sister, why do you whisper, and won't you tell me where you've been?
Stand off, stand off, you bloody butchers, my love and I you have both slain.

ENDING

▶LYRICS—POLLY ON THE SHORE

INTRO

1. Come all of you wild young men
   And a warning take by me,
   Never to lead your single life astray
   Into no bad company.

2. As I myself have done
   Being in the merry month of May,
   When I was pressed by a sea captain
   And on board a man-of-war I did go.
   When I was pressed by a sea captain
   And on board a man-of-war I did go.

3. We sailed on the ocean so blue
   And our bonny, bonny flag we let fly,
   Let every man stand true to his guns
   For the Lord knows who must die.
   Let every man stand true to his guns
   For the Lord knows who must die.

4. Our captain was wounded full sore,
   So were the best of his men,
   Our mainmast rigging lay a-scattered on the deck
   And so we were obliged to give in.
   Our mainmast rigging lay a-scattered on the deck
   And so we were obliged to give in.

   BREAK

5. Our decks they were spattered with blood,
   So loudly the cannons did roar,
   And many's the time have I wished myself at home
   All along with my Polly on the shore.

6. She's a fair and a tender girl,
   She's a dark and a rolling eye,
   And here am I lie bleeding on the deck
   And for her sweet sake I shall die.
   Here am I lie bleeding on the deck
   And for her sweet sake I shall die.

7. Farewell to my parents and my friends,
   Farewell to my dear Polly too,
   I never should have rambled the salt sea so wide
   If I had been ruled by you.
   I never should have rambled the salt sea so wide
   If I had been ruled by you.

   ENDING

APPENDIX—SUMMARY OF TUNINGS

Open D—Page 12

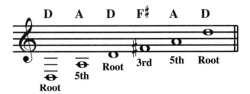

Open D High Equivalent Open E—Page 12

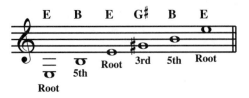

Open G—Page 16

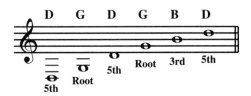

Open C—Page 22

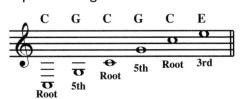

Open C High Equivalent Open D—Page 22

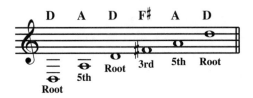

DADGAD—Page 26

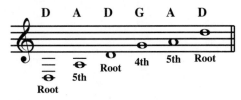

Gsus4—Page 30

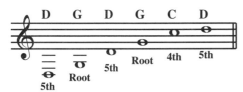

D Minor—Page 32

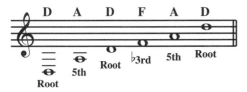

Open G Minor—Page 33

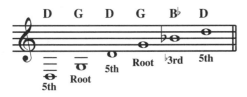

Open C Minor—Page 33

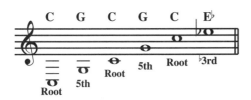

Csus2 or Cadd9—Page 35

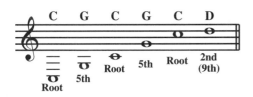

Csus4—Page 36

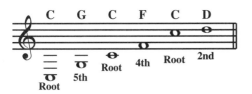

Gsus4/4—Page 56

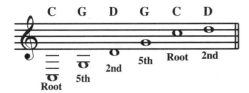